i

TWENTY NINE POEMS BY AN ALIEN

Twenty nine poems by an alien. A social study of life, employment and education on Earth. Through the poetry of Dr Nebulas Zorg.
© Starry Eyed Publishing, 2014.

ISBN 978-0-9575480-2-2

Twitter: @nebulaszorg
Facebook: NebulasZorg
www.nebulaszorg.com
nebulaszorg@gmail.com

TWENTY NINE POEMS BY AN ALIEN: A SOCIAL STUDY OF LIFE, EMPLOYMENT AND EDUCATION ON EARTH THROUGH THE POETRY OF DR NEBULAS ZORG

CONTENTS

	ABOUT THE AUTHOR	Page 1
1.	EVOLUTION	Page 5
2.	STEERAGE	Page 8
3.	POLL TAX	Page 12
4.	TWO LANDS	Page 13
5.	REALITY	Page 16
6.	BEING BORN	Page 17
7.	SONG OF THE EARTH	Page 19
8.	LATIN REQUIEM	Page 21
9.	COUNTDOWN	Page 23
10.	UNANSWERED EMAIL	Page 24
11.	THE POETRY CRITIC	Page 26
12.	WINTER	Page 27
13.	THIS BE THE COST	Page 30
14.	THE FOE	Page 33
15.	THE SUBURBS	Page 34
16.	THE FAT CAPITALIST	Page 36
17.	WITNESS	Page 38
18.	THE THREE Rs	Page 40
19.	THE CAREERS MASTER	Page 41
20.	DIRECTIONS	Page 43
21.	IRONY	Page 45
22.	DEFORESTATION	Page 46
23.	THE STRING	Page 47
24.	DRESS CODE	Page 48
25.	LARKIN' ABOUT	Page 49
26.	WISHFUL THINKING	Page 51
27.	THE GREAT DIVIDER	Page 53
28.	BASE METALS	Page 54
29.	YOU LOST ME AT HELLO	Page 55
	EPILOGUE	Page 57

About the author: Dr Nebulas Zorg

Little is known about the author, Dr Nebulas Zorg. It is believed that he first entered the world in the early 1960s and from that day has sought to understand the complexities of planet Earth, through the mediums of education, employment and social science research – the latter being a 'doss subject', according to his maker.

He remembers, at the age of four Earth years, attending his first Earth school in a nondescript council estate in the suburbs. His teacher painfully knuckled him in the back every day, whilst spewing saliva and eruptingly expectorating the phrase "get on with your work and face the front you little sod." He remembers little else about the school, where he spent the next six Earth years. These were the fascinating 'formative years' of his upbringing where he learned "absolutely bugger all at school except what complete c***s some people can be."

The author graduated through the 'Eleven Plus' system; an Earth-constructed educational system designed to sort the 'wheat' from the 'chaff', and attended 'Meaningless Grammar' – a school renowned for its draconian corporal punishment regime. Here, in the white heat of a 'first-class educational establishment', he lovingly reports learning that he had now become a "stupid pleb" in Physics; an "idiotic peasant" in English; a "stupid, stupid, stupid boy" in Maths; "utterly, utterly hopeless" in History; an "all time moron" in Chemistry, and his personal favourite; a "complete cretin" in Latin. His French teacher wrote of him "he has an even worse grasp of this subject this year than he did last year." In Music, even though the author was by now an accomplished pianist, he learned the phrase "look you fucking idiot, just leave the fucking piano alone will you. It's locked for a reason – so that it doesn't get broken." He tells me that he never did get to play the school piano.

During these grammar school years, Dr Nebulas tells me that he realised that his early years impressions of what complete c***s people could be, were now reinforced. At this school though, the author did learn that cricket and rugby were "pretty much the same" in that in both sports, a whole load of boys ran around chasing a ball, with staff and players shouting defamatory remarks about anyone that was near it. Here he learned from the Physical Education – or 'PE' staff (ripplingly muscled and fit, younger men with shorts so tight that their voices gained a whole 2.6 octaves above the other staff) the helpful phrases, "Look, you c**t, just pass the fucking ball you fucking idiot", and, "You fucking, fucking stupid gobshite, why did you not pass the ball to silly mid off?" Phrases he thought would be most useful in his later alien life.

Dr Nebulas then ventured out into the world of higher education, attending the London School of Economics as both a graduate and (surprisingly) – considering, as he put it, his "fucking useless Grammar School education" – as a PhD student. Here, at this "wonderfully mystical place" he tells me, he learned many, many things from other aliens who knew many, many things – and who were just like him. He found his God – Dionysus– and he learned what it meant to be an INTJ adrift in a world of Apollonians. In subjects called Psychology and Politics he learned about the Earth Goddess; about people and places, and he tried – but failed – to discover what it is that makes most people the complete c***s that he had found them generally to be.

He also discovered what it took to make a 16 topping pizza including (of course), banana and corned beef – a skill known only to an honoured few on the fourth floor of the LSE. And, I am given to understand, a skill that has now been lost to mankind.

This LSE and, in particular, the Beaver Bar and the Three Tuns, were special places of sanctuary for aliens; mostly safe from a world of complete and utter bastards. In fact, whenever any bastard Earthling secretly tried to gain access to the hallowed halls of the LSE, he says, they were told to fuck off. The Three Tuns, Dr Nebulas informs me, he believes is a reference to the quantity of beer consumed on a normal Friday night by the Social Psychology department.

Out of a desire for greater knowledge of the wider species, our author also ventured out into the world of employment, taking on any challenges, and undertaking any journey – no matter how far, and at whatever cost – to glimpse a vista of what normal people do in this world. He didn't like what he saw, and decided that it was only through the medium of poetry that he could document his travels and experiences.

The author tells me that, amongst other things, during his time on Earth, he has been: an assistant chemist, factory machinist, pilot, researcher, carer, writer, photographer, poet, teacher, university lecturer, cartographer, geologist, GIS consultant, cleaner, tactical systems developer, designer, risk analyst, operations specialist, archaeologist and police officer. And for many years he spent his time in the military; learning how, being armed with the minimum amount of resources, he could deploy limited sphere tactical weaponry to get away with killing the maximum number of people in the minimum amount of time. Useful skills, he feels, to have in a world full of complete bastards.

It was during these years, though, that Dr Nebulas found a soulmate; a wonderful, wonderful alien hailing from an alternative alien world. But this alien was different. She was brilliant; she knew about music and art and language and she knew how to get the very best out of Earthlings – and most especially how to get the very best out of the author. She was one who cared for all mankind. This was a very special person indeed. Dr Nebulas says that his world is lucky to have her here, and our author has struck a lifelong alliance and TEAM with this alien. This alien is the love of our author's life.

By complete and lucky coincidence, though, the author tells me that in hailing from a planet with ever-so-slightly less gravity than that on Earth, Dr Nebulas is in fact quite tall, whereas 'love-of-his-life' soulmate is in fact ever-so-slightly more vertically challenged. Dr Nebulas has therefore taken to heart the phrase, "Bloody hell, why did you have to have the kitchen cupboards up so high? Reach me down the ruddy pesto!" Equally though, the author felt that it was fortuitistic indeed to have an ever-so-slightly more vertically challenged TEAM member around when he was recently unable to take a photograph of his right foot. This is indeed a happy alliance.

This lifelong alliance with the author's soul mate has beget two other aliens. A boy alien and a girl alien. Both are aliens of attitude. They are complex, capable, intelligent and entirely independent subjects who have themselves learned that the world is full of utter bastards. But they are aliens who are survivors – able to command, able to compete, able to succeed and able to blend into this world – and they have begun their own journeys of discovery. The author is phenomenally proud of both of these aliens and he pities any Earthling who crosses them.

The author currently resides with his wonderful alien soulmate and his time lord canine companion in a humble dwelling in the stockbroker belt of London, where he spends most of his time writing poetry, teaching, photographing and researching; with a bit of shopping online, and of course trying, as he puts it, "not to talk to too many people."

Please be aware that there is (necessary) profanity in this book.

Ever aware of the need for 21st century gratuitous self promotion and advertising, Dr Nebulas tells me that Earthlings may like to follow his research on:

Twitter: @nebulaszorg
Facebook: NebulasZorg
or via his website: www.nebulaszorg.com
or indeed they may email him on: nebulaszorg@gmail.com

Although Dr Nebulas does point out that his email system is set by default to divert everything straight into the trash because, as he succinctly puts it, he really "can't be arsed to communicate with anyone as, by and large they're complete c***s anyway."

1. EVOLUTION

Dr Nebulas spent several years studying climate change, pollution and the technocentric fallacy. No idea why, just that everyone seemed to be harping on about it. Tree huggers; academics wanting to extend their research grants; politicians wanting to tax cow farts; that sort of thing.

He realised that, for the first four and a half thousand million years, the Earth did just fine without 'Man'. Admittedly, it was a bit hot on occasions, and a bit chilly on others. But, by and large, most living stuff survived most of the time; most stuff evolved happily.

Although there were a few shaky moments when the odd bollide struck the Earth at a billion miles an hour or something, causing some aitken nucleii, dust and gas to be ejected to great heights. This then irritatingly reflected ultraviolet short wave energy into the upper troposphere and stratosphere, making it both very chilly indeed, and ever-so-slightly unpleasant for any Earth creature that hadn't planned for this contingency. This, combined with several billion tonnes of sulphur dioxide erupting from super volcanoes 'did it in' for a few species that had been around for three hundred million years or so.

Then, of course, out of the gloop, Man came along. And in the geologic blink of an eye that is the quaternary, Man has rather made a mess of things. Deforestation, pollution, water depletion, greenhouse gases, expansive monoculture, and of course, bankers. But not to worry! If we broke it, they say, we can fix it....or maybe not, we're really not too sure about that one... Dr Nebulas wonders what the Earth would have been like without Man here at all...

If Man had evolved into a new type of spinach,
Where would the planet be now?
Instead of commuters and super computers,
The land might be covered in cows.

The seas would have cities of porpoise and purpose,
And humans just wouldn't be found.
The forests would flourish, and animals nourish,
On the plentiful greenstuff around.

The rivers would ripple, the hummingbirds tipple,
The nectar untouched by our hand.
The lions would tower, and wildebeest cower,
And the coasts would be virgin white sand.

But what of the warning, of planetary warming?
What would happen if 'We' were not there?
Without mechanisation, or industrialisation,
To place chemicals high in the air?

Instead of peroxide, and carbon monoxide,
The air would be fresh and appealing,
Hover flies hover, without any bother,
And the pigs would be squeaking and squealing.

But hold on! Cows pass, from their several stomachs,
A majestic concoction of gas.
In litres a-plenty, comes methane, quite gently,
But in quantities sufficient to mass.

With the troposphere choking, and Savannah lands smoking,
From the fires now caused by the sun,
In the equatorial heat, all species retreat,
Without ever sighting a gun.

Without us, a planet to ravage and ruin,
Is hardly a Utopian dream.
How could it survive, without Man alive,
To meddle and make a machine?

That can save all the creatures, can cure all the problems,
Of a planet that's rapidly dying.
It's time to put right, all the things that we might,
Have destroyed, without really trying.

Without us to plunder, and pillage, and blunder,
Our way to a new found solution,
Landscapes would survive, under different skies,
But isn't that just Evolution?

2. STEERAGE

Dr Nebulas once spent several unpleasant Earth years working as a teacher – gaining 'valuable' experience in a range of schools. In a class structure assessment not so dissimilar from Dunleavy's Consumption Cleavages, Neb, as he is often called by his close colleagues, categorises these educational institutions as: 1) 'Private' – high fees, low brain power; where the students think that sex is what coal comes in. 2) 'State' – no fees and staff who "rock on down, dude," wear jeans and Bob Marley T-shirts, and where Earthlings are forced to remain for most of their adolescent life so that, as one highly experienced Earth teacher put it, "the little bastards are kept off the streets, and out of crime for a decade." 3) 'Public Schools' – ultra-high fees and students with ponies, and who often look like ponies.

Here, Neb tells me, he learned from a year 9 student (year 9 students, for those that don't know, are sullen, moody, dishevelled, opinionated scrawny little brats with ponies called Arrabella and Hector) the phrase, "your tie, eee Dr Zorg clearly cost you all of threee euros, whereas weee have a 7-Series BMW."

Furthermore, Dr Nebulas experienced 'sixth form colleges' – places attended by students who have failed to remain at their chosen educational institution because: 1) they have failed to gain the requisite G grade at GCSE, or 2) (and more likely) they don't actually want to learn anything anyway. It was at one of these colleges that Dr Nebulas learned the phrase, "look, just sod off, why are you bothering me? I'm having a doze, I was up most of the night partying and then threw up in the taxi." Dr Nebulas also found that the students were not any better. As part of his social science research at one institution, Dr Nebulas discovered the famous Dilbert Principle; the concept of staff being promoted beyond the level of their competence...

First, take a school in a fabulous location,
Where pupils return happy after every vacation.
This in itself is an enviable trait,
And the staff are happy and pull their own weight.

New buildings develop, resources abound,
And all round the school, smiling faces are found.
Smiling students, smiling teachers, support staff and cleaners,
There's rarely a punishment; there are few misdemeanours.

I wouldn't say it's idyllic, but it's really not bad,
The results just delivered are the best ever had.
Top school in the tables, top school by miles,
Could it really be down to hard-working teachers and smiles?

Not according to the Head, who's just been appointed,
From a questioning deputy, to One Now Anointed.
It's all down to the students, you see, for helping each other,
The staff don't do anything, they really don't bother.

The Head can't stop talking about this thing and that,
Spending days droning on about the fate of a cat,
That seemed to be lost in the car park outside,
The Head was, of course, the one to deal with it and decide.

The staff, the Head broadcasts, are all skivers and slackers,
They make no contribution, but what really matters,
Is that the Head is the only one who works in this school,
The staff are just lazy; they don't work at all...

Having gained the promotion to demi-god status,
The Head now controls every school apparatus.
Try to change the bog roll from off-pink to white?
We wouldn't be able; because we couldn't do it right.

9

Only the Head had the power and awe-inspired vision,
To make any small change, any minor decision.
While the staff sit and despair, and ponder anew,
And the Head sits on leather, and considers a review.

A review of the useless staff and the way,
They witter and complain, and waste every day.
Time that they should be teaching, and working away,
Time that they've been overpaid for; a review of their pay?

I know more than you, says the Head, because I'm the Head.
I know better than you, says the Head, because I'm the Head.
I know things you don't, says the Head, because I'm the Head.
You know nothing says the Head, you're a slacker, says the
Head, I know, says the Head, because
I'm the Head, says the Head.

How did this sorry state come about,
That this Head was appointed when the advert went out?
It was a Head that was wanted, with all sensibilities,
Not a tyrant and bully promoted beyond capabilities.

I don't know about the process to appoint and select,
But it doesn't take Einstein or Sherlock to detect,
That it might have been better to promote a Head who's brainy,
Than one who is arrogant, rude and meglomanie.

The school steams full ahead through the ice and the fog,
Whilst the Head now promotes every little lap dog.
Like an emperor's new clothes, or a ship all at sea,
Er, what sort of sycophant,
Head, would you like me to be?

Again and again, it's what we all dread.
One staff member even mentioned it would be better to be dead,
Than to be in the office and hear the Head repeat all that was said.
Why say in ten words, what can be said in ten thousand instead?

To my mind it ruined a job that I loved,
A school and community that I rated above,
The others I've worked at, in a career of good standing,
The Head that has done this without understanding.

The damage that's been done taking a visionary prance,
With car crash finesse and a myopic stance,
That wouldn't be questioned or challenged by anyone bold,
The Head's the Head, AND better than everyone else;
we're repeatedly told.

I've left, like so many others (I hear),
Some others have gone, the remainder just fear,
That the Head is steering them all to disaster,
And the ship will be lost with all souls ever after.

3. POLL TAX

Dr Nebulas, during his London School of Economics crusade years, discovered that there were being sold ill-fitting 'Bollocks to the Poll Tax' T-shirts in nearby Covent Garden. He was presented with one of these as a reward for his considerable team-work contribution on the Fishum Theory – a little-known theory appertaining to, but in fact not-at-all-directly-related-to, the workings of our nearest star. This he wore with pride and then spent many happy days with his alien friends wandering up and down Kingsway like it meant something and it was, in any case, infinitely preferable to attending Philosophy lectures.

If gases were rationed, and politics fashioned
Into policies environmentally green,
Emissions would be leaner;
The atmosphere cleaner,
And politicians, far less obscene.

Whilst the ozone is thinning,
The councils are twinning
With towns that are pointless to know.
Instead of a jolly, invest-all-the-lolly
In a sustainable future-to-go!

INVOICE

Sustainable
future

£X.XX

4. TWO LANDS

Dr Nebulas, by way of empirical analysis, once lived in a house that was next to a river. It was lovely; a horse called Hector lived in the field opposite, and no-one ever visited. Neb was very happy here. However, the house occasionally flooded. What Neb did, though, was to buy his own sandbags and door seals. Then, when the water rose, he would happily move everything upstairs until the water went away and clear up the mess afterwards. Flooding's a bummer, he felt, but then again, he reasoned that he did choose to live by a river.

Nebby realised that there are a lot of floods around the world, but few that we all get to hear about. The important ones – the really, really, really, really, really important ones are of course the ones that affect...who?

There were once two lands;
The land of the clinging, and
The land of the whingeing.
Both lands were suffering.

In the land of the clinging,
Rising waters forced a whole population
To cling to the roofs of their makeshift houses,
Whilst their lives were carried away
In a torrent of sad acceptance.

The floods have come early this year.

In the land of the whingeing,
Rising waters forced a whole community
To cling to their phones, in their permanent homes,
Whilst their hours were carried away
In a torrent of abuse and complaint.

The floods shouldn't happen to Us.

In the land of the clinging, they stay.
No one comes to pay.
Or reimburse their loss and their suffering.
Who cares about their pathetic lives?
Why do they live there anyway?

Say the people in the land of the whingeing, where

They move to ground that is higher and drier
To ease their suffering.
Who cares about their important lives?
WHO has allowed THIS to happen?

They say.

In the land of the clinging,
Life is held by fingertips,
Or dies.
Unseen.
Grasping at straws.

Nothing is said.

In the land of the whingeing, what trauma exists?
How can they live without the record collection?
Unheard for so long.
But now worth more,
Than all the years of toil and unrewarded decades
In the land of the clinging.

No, in the land of the whingeing
The value is clear.
And worth more.
Much more.
Than those in the land of the clinging can ever imagine.

They say.

In the land of the whingeing
Reimbursement is met with a derisory tone.
It's seldom the real value.
It's never enough,
Or what it's worth.
As they return to their
Permanence.

In the land of the clinging
Few are left to rebuild from their watery tombs.
The strands of life that remain
Clinging to a landscape of disease.
It's what they have.
It's all they have.
As they cling.

5. REALITY

Dr Nebulas realises that he has observed many people who tell him that they have a vision for the way that they – and others, even if they don't want to do so – should live. These people are often called politicians.

I had a dream!
No.
I didn't really.

6. BEING BORN

Well, it has to happen. There you are one day unhappily concocted onto Planet Zorg and from that moment on, you're screwed. No choice. You might think that you command your destiny, but you don't. Admittedly you do get to choose whether you buy a 42-inch plasma instead of an organic LED. No, wait, you can't afford an organic LED anyway. In two hundred years time, readers, you, like Dr Nebulas, will all be history.

Incidentally, Dr Nebulas did study History in his formative years at Meaningless Grammar, although 'study' is a loose term. Dr Nebulas never actually saw the face of his History teacher, as for the whole five Earth years, his History teacher faced the chalkboard and wrote indecipherable notes on the board shouting, "writ this all down will yee", whilst paper aeroplanes and tiny pieces of folded paper pinged by elastic bands flew around the room behind him. Dr Nebulas obliged with the History 'note taking', but at the end of his Grammar School years his notes made no sense and, wondering to himself what all this shit was, he burnt them.

You don't choose when
You don't choose where
You don't choose your name
You don't choose your hair

You don't choose your colour
You don't choose your skin
You don't choose the accent
Of the country you're in

You don't choose the time
You don't choose the place
You don't choose your beauty
Or the ugliest face

For some it's so simple
For some it's a fight
For some it's unfairness
For some it's a right

It's your fault you're out there
It's your fault you're wrong
It's all so insincere
As you're carried along

On a wave of resentment
A journey of tears
You don't choose your freedom
You don't choose the years

That you've spent choosing nothing
But people to hate
For some it's all over.
You don't choose your fate.

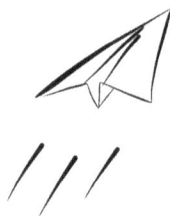

7. SONG OF THE EARTH

After many years of isolation, living among seven billion people,
Dr Nebulas realised that his quest for knowledge – an alien on
an alien world – was going to add up to nothing more than an
echo waiting to strike a non-existent distant wall.

Forget that I have lived. Forget that I have given.

When you feel the warmth of sunlight passing across golden
leaves,
Rejoice that you are alive.
Sunlight on water,
reflecting on life;
reflecting on past lives.
illuminating achievement and growth; yet

In the shadow of the Oak, the dimness exposes a wealth of
hard work,
and effort,
unrewarded by the rays of light,
like the slow passage of time
along a disused railway,
where once great achievements thundered by.

Forget that I have lived. Forget that I have given.

Now is gone and nothing remains of value, that ever stood
and tried to be counted;
or heard
with all the impact of a passing stone that is thrown,
but fails ever to strike a target.
A meteorite, which is forever alone.

Forget that I have lived. Forget that I have given.

What were your ancestors like? Were they good? Were they
funny?
Did they care
about the colour of the sky, or the water passing by?
Did they love
the smell of the earth, or the warmth of friendship?
Remember them.

Forget that I have lived. Forget that I have given.

I was really not here.
Like sunlight passing into space;
never to warm the Earth
or fall on fields of green
but to pass in silence, into space
unseen.

8. LATIN REQUIEM

This poem is one of Dr Nebulas' favourites. It is set within the author's formative alien years at Meaningless Grammar School. A Grammar School, for those that don't know, is just like a 'Private School' (see 'Steerage' above) but no-one owns a horse. And even if they did, it would be called Trigger, not Arabella or Hector.

Here, Dr Nebulas mastered the language of Latin with the help of his outstanding Latin educator; believed by many to be a close cousin of Nero. Latin was not so much a subject that you learned progressively, but rather one that you learned painfully. Latin, Dr Nebulas felt, would be extremely useful in later life when he was attending future Erasmus courses and wanted half price alcohol.

Today I looked through my old school reports.
Latin: unsatisfactory progress.
A poor grasp of the subject.
This child is a true cretin.

But thirty years on, what report do I give my Master?
Coldness, cruelty, unforgiving.
Echoing, lonely and distant.
Uncaring and bullying.

The Latin teacher who called me 'cretin'
Was an ignominious bully.
Behind his back I would call him a bastard.
I don't remember his name; just Pinky the fat bastard.

He thought it was funny to frighten
A class full of cretins.
With his fiery breath,
Halitosis from years of uncleaned, ochre-stained teeth.

Pinky had a miniature guillotine
Which he would parade to the class.
And with it, cut sticks of chalk in half.
Metal slicing calcium.

Then he would force a cretin's finger into the machine,
And bellow and threaten
The same fate as the chalk, to our calcium joints
If we did not conjugate the verb.

As my fingers trembled, did I learn to conjugate the verb?
I was learning how to loathe.
I was learning how to fear.
I was learning how to hate.

He taught me what it was like to be bullied and battered,
He taught me how to duck to avoid missiles hurled
With torrents of abuse.
Because of incorrectly conjugated verbs.

And now? Do I look back affectionately, and say,
Ah, good old Pinky the Latin teacher.
He never did me any harm; he toughened me up,
Taught me a thing or two, the old blighter.

Do I now laughingly conjugate verbs
And quote Latin texts,
And think
There was reason in his madness?

No. Thirty years on I think him less than a bastard.
He taught me what it was like to be taught by a cretin.
Like his language
I hope he is dead.

9. COUNTDOWN

Dr Nebulas has discovered that Man is polluting the planet at a rate faster than a Zorgian Muffet can urinate; something similar to a cross between a pressurised water nuclear reactor and a wart hog. Dr Nebulas fears the worst for Earth. "Many years ago," he says, "the Earth used to be a nice place to live." "Now," he says, succinctly, "the planet's fucked, man."

Is dilution the solution to pollution?

If,

Pollution, creation
Recreation, desecration
Ruination, apprehension
Solution, dilution

but,

Pollution, dilution
Creation, apprehension
Solution, recreation

however,

Dilution, solution
Creation, desecration

therefore,

Apprehension, ruination.

10. UNANSWERED EMAIL

It happens to everyone. Everyone that is, of a 'certain age'. There you are happily browsing through your copy of Motorcycle News looking for a new warp speed machine that can whisk alien and 'love-of-his-life' alien across continents, to far-flung romantic destinations, when email starts arriving from colleagues whom you have not seen or heard of for decades. And all they can think about is some fucking reunion. Honestly. Why?

Why on Earth do Earthlings seem to want to dress up in their old fucking cub scout or school uniforms and re-live (Oh Joy...) those shitty, piss-awful days which, quite frankly, were not so good anyway.

Most of the Earthlings he has ever met, Dr Nebulas hasn't liked; and those that he did like, he didn't like for very long. "Most people are complete c***s" he says, "I didn't like meeting them in the first place, so why o' why would I want to have the vastly unpleasant experience of meeting them all over again?"

Hey! Come and join in the old school website!
All your friends are on it – it'll be great!
Hey! Come and join in the old school reunion!
All those friends, that I once used to hate.

You can tell your lacrosse team how successful your life's been!
You can publish the fact you're a star!
You can let em' all know that you're richer than they are!
And joke that they said, you'll go far!

You can exchange all those memories of teachers and lessons!
And chat to your buddies of old!
But, exchange all my memories of encounter group sessions?
And share stories I never want told?

We've already passed around your number and details!
So that your colleagues can 'e' for a chat!
There's Brummer and Happy – they've signed up already!
And so has old Stinky (the prat)!

I don't want any part of my old school website.
Menopausal mates whom I continue to resent.
I don't want my photos and stories unpleasant,
Displayed twenty years on to present;

Me, as I am now; not me as I was, then;
No website could ever explain
All the successes and failures my life has been full of,
And I can't live my life once again.

11. THE POETRY CRITIC

Dr Nebulas recognises the fact that not every Earthling appreciates classy poetry...

If you don't fucking like it,
Then don't fucking read it.
It's not your fucking poem.
So fuck off.

Still reading?

So, if you do like the poem
but don't like the swearing,
Some folk might think you're a toff.
You may be a lawyer, a teacher, or banker,
Some others might think you're a bit of a wanker.
So like I said in the first place;
Fuck off.

12. WINTER

In his voyage of discovery around planet Earth, Dr Nebulas has interviewed many people of all ages, colours and creeds. Many people on this planet are older than others, he says. And often these elder states-people have fought in wars, survived famines, floods, pain and discomfort; and have even survived eating at fast food outlets that have poor hygiene records.

These people are, he says, the stalwarts of society, who have so much experience and knowledge, but who are so often overlooked and ignored. These people often live in bleak seaside towns and shuffle along the streets, but you don't see them, even though they are there.

White cliffs and bungalows
With cherry-red doors and emerald roofs
Peer out under nimbostratus skies,
And stare apprehensively out to sea.

An icy chill is kept just at bay
By mufflers and scarves unwrapped from cellophane,
Stored safely since a long-forgotten birthday.
One of so many uncounted for so long.

A battle begins; to fight the cold, to fight the old
With few allies, and many enemies.
There's a new strain of flu this year,
Virulent and malicious; or so I hear.

Sinuous lines and wrinkled queues form for hypodermics of
Anti-this and anti-that.
It's not like it used to be.
In the old days, we knew how to behave, knew how to look
after our seniors.

There will be no injections
Of much needed cash,
From people keen to help those we do not forget.
Policies address much more important matters of state.

For some reason this is going to be a tough season.
Do they know it's going to be their last season?
Just as it was last year,
When the leaves had fallen.

Every day, every short, wheeled basket walk
Is to get bread and milk, and talk,
Of past achievements, past lives,
And impending unease.

Every outing is met by a barrage of coldness,
Stronger and more potent than the last,
Which seems to tear at the sinews
As it percolates every cellophane-unwrapped new layer.

Behind cherry doors, the heat reduces, ever so gently,
To conserve, not energy, as the latest posters say,
But dwindling reserves
Of finances not insulated from unseasonal bitterness.

A degree or two lower, a penny or two less to drain away,
Life itself becomes a balancing act;
Between consciousness and capital.
If only we could hibernate.

Stock up, eat cake, jam tomorrow.
They've heard all the phrases;
Unfulfilling euphemistic political morsels
Which nourish no one, and leave a bitter after taste.

They've heeded all the advice, they really have.
They sit with ulcerated legs in plastic sacks,
To guard against the draught caused by ill-fitting panes
Installed by the heirloom auctioned for all its worth.

The old guard only heats the room they are in.
But why bother? It would be very cheap to die.
Think of all the pennies saved
By not having any warmth at all.

As the political temperature soars
At conferences with bottled water and marble floors,
The long slow descent begins for those with thick socks
And hot water bottles that have never been charged.

These are the battalions who smile through it all.
It'll be all right, they say.
We'll be OK.
Best foot forward, can't complain.

These are the soldiers who won a war
But are about to lose the final battle.
Mustn't grumble.
Winter is here.

13. THIS BE THE COST

By way of diversion from his busy alien life, Dr Nebulas entered the teaching profession for a number of years and taught in many Earth schools; as his c.v puts it, "to gain valuable experience in an range of educational establishments." In reality, Dr Nebulas was simply gaining empirical research material in disbelief that any school he moved to could be worse than the school he'd just left.

Like himself, Dr Nebulas discovered, Earth teachers work a thirty seven-hour day, largely compressed into twenty four Earth hours either by having an association with a time lord canine companion, or cheap Tequila.

Eight hours for lesson preparation, assuming that anyone in the class is going to pay attention anyway. Three hours for travelling. Eight hours standing in front of a class of thirty five disenfranchised fifteen year-old Earthlings with only thirty chairs available as some were broken and some had been thrown out of the window.

Dr Nebulas says that he spent almost all of the latter eight hours ('contact time') repeating the mantra, "Sit down, Wayne", "Sit Down Wayne", "SIT Down Wayne", "SIT DOWN Wayne", "SIT DOWN WAYNE." Seven hours for marking; using a red pen to write, "this is excellent Wayne, but the answer would be even better if it related to the tectonic plates, and not your cousin." Three hours for sleeping. Three hours for lying awake in bed wondering if the little sods are going to stuff mud up your motorcycle exhaust pipe again. And five hours drinking Tequila from a plastic cup so that no one notices.

Every Earth teacher Dr Nebulas has known has managed to

achieve this thirty seven/twenty four-hour time compression miracle. But then again, Dr Nebulas considered, Earth teachers always bugger off at 3.15pm every day and have phenomenally long holidays, so they should stop bitching...

At one Earth educational establishment, Dr Nebulas recalls crowd controlling a pack of said 'disenfranchised' sixteen-year old Earthlings; one of whom the Modern Languages staff affectionately called 'Cupcakes'. Dr Nebulas' mission was to help this Earthling achieve its 'full potential', which was a tricky task indeed as the Earthling had clearly already reached that.

Dr Nebulas: "so, is it in the east or the west?" Cupcakes: "in the west". Dr Nebulas: "try another." Cupcakes: "er.... east?" Dr Nebulas: "well done, Earthling." Dr Nebulas: "so, please can anyone explain the transfer of short and long wave energy through the aspect of the solar radiation window?" Cupcakes, with hand held proudly aloft: "No."

Dr Nebulas once went with this pack on a field course. A field course, for the non-teaching Earthlings, is where knackered teachers take entire packs of disenfranchised little sods to a study centre (the clue is in the name) where they then spend a week apologising to study centre staff members for the broken glass panels and the fire alarm going off in the middle of the night.

Earthling headteachers consider field courses to be a valuable part of the curriculum. Earthling students, on the other hand, consider field courses to be fabulous opportunities to meet with Earthling students of the opposite sex, and then spend the rest of the week conjuring up ways to get laid.

Here, Cupcakes realised that being left in a group on a hillside to do field work was a euphemism for getting a taxi to the nearest pub to get pissed, then getting a taxi back at pick up time, then presenting Dr Nebulas with hastily scribbled notes describing some influence of cheese shops in a rural hamlet. There were, of course, no cheese shops. And so the null hypothesis, of course, had to be accepted.

Dr Nebulas' own formative years' experiences as a student at Meaningless Grammar did in fact stand him in good stead here and, later in life, Dr Nebulas encouraged Cupcakes to get a job in a mobile phone shop.

They rip you off, those mobile phones,
And they mean to. Yes they do.
They charge you for extra polyphonic tones,
And add a personal alert just for you.

Sold by faceless people who, in their turn,
Rip off customers dressed in multicoloured coats.
Who half the time, have no mind to learn
And all the time at one another's throats.

Confusion marketing, a parasitic plan,
You see them on the shopfront shelf.
Learn to avoid the salesman;
Don't buy a mobile phone yourself.

14. THE FOE

Alien inspiration comes in many guises. Dr Nebulas tells me that he doesn't actually remember the creative juices that flowed to write this poem. He does, however, remember one night consuming a couple of bottles of Paarl Valley Pinotage before picking up his pen and clipboard. The next day he awoke with an idea for a poem from his 'kraken' headache.

Who goes there? Friend or foe?
The kraken – a friend.
How do we know that you are a friend, kraken?
I bring riches and gifts of perfume and silk.
Do these gifts make you a friend, kraken?
The gifts are mere baubles, my friendship the riches.
Am I to enter then, gatekeeper? Or do I pass by?
Pass by then, kraken. We have no need of your riches here.

15. THE SUBURBS

In the 1960s, when Dr Nebulas first began his social research into life, employment and education on Earth, he came across the words 'status' and 'prestige'. These are strange words indeed, mused Dr Nebulas.

Words often used in parallel with phrases such as 'upper, lower or working class', "well really, what will the neighbours think?" and "next door's doorstep is dirtier than ours." Dr Nebulas found that anybody who *is anybody* would have to work in the most prestigious place of all; the City. No job in the City, no status.

Hey, I've just found the most wonderful job around.
I'll be working in unit trusts in a nearby provincial town.
It's close and convenient – and there's no need to commute
To the congested City where there's no good bus route.

Not work in the City? But in a town in the 'shires'?
What's happened to your thinking? Is this all to which you aspire?
With status and position, a City job is best.
And think of our poor neighbours
– their imagination will do the rest.

The City means you've made it. It means you're something.
The underclass will respect you and afford your every imposition.
Not a failure, in the suburbs; some carrot-crunching community,
But a manager with white collar and suit
– and who fires with impunity.

An embarrassment to your family if you settle for mediocrity.
A provincial job in the shires; they'll all laugh
– despite your seniority.
Where's your bulldog drive? Where's your killing spirit?
They all have it in the City.
A provincial job in the suburbs? You'll be looked upon with pity.

Where's the logic in all this self-delusion and ideal
Where the people who work in cities, who have made it.
What appeals?
Standing in carriages. We'll sue you for damages!
WE are shopping in Claridge's.
It's all an illusion, an icon of stupidity and pride.
The City is not a solution.

16. THE FAT CAPITALIST

During the course of Dr Nebulas' Economics research, he discovered that the value of an Earthling's working day is not the same for everyone.

An Earthling's worth will be considerably more if it finds itself able to push a ball around successfully and stick a certain 'un in the net,' and 'clean up a game'; than an Earthling who successfully pushes a broom around and just 'cleans up.'

The value of a successful ball person's day is about £59,988, whereas the successful broom-pushing person's day is valued at about £56. The successful ball-pushing person does, though, have to work on Saturdays; so maybe this is the difference?

If I were a Marxist, I don't think I'd have
Such capital worth; and an XK8 Jag.

I wouldn't have all those trappings that come
From a life of debauchery, inequality and fun.

But why should I care as a capitalist I,
If others have nothing to eat or get by.

They should be getting a good job – those peasants and paupers
Instead of disturbing our doorsteps as hawkers.

Instead of sleeping on pavements and in doorways
They should get off their arses. There have got to be more ways.

To get them some money – and they should earn their own living
Instead of a handout from people forgiving.

Their slovenly ways and their shoddy attire.
I'll keep all my cash, thanks, I need my stash to retire.

17. WITNESS

During Dr Nebulas' formative years he lived for a time in what is colloquially called, a 'shite London overspill council estate.' Here he spent many unhappy years partaking in the daily ritual of dodging the air-gun pellets fired by some complete c***s, as he puts it, on the estate on his way back from Meaningless First School. They were in some way fucked off that he and others were walking past their fucking house. You fucking bastards.

One resident, Dr Nebulas noted, was not quite as quick as he at dodging pellets and was, in fact, hospitalised; felled unconscious with a pellet lodged in his skull. Dr Nebulas remembers to this day the copious volumes of blood flowing down the pavement, into the road and gutter and towards the drain. Head wounds do bleed a lot, he found out, especially if you happen to have been shot...

The bloodstain on the pavement lingered for weeks after this and Dr Nebulas put a great deal of effort into honing his pellet-dodging skills and reflexes – useful skills for use in later military life.

So, saddened by the findings of his social study of life in his immediate surroundings, Dr Nebulas instead turned his attention to the wider world, where he mused, "just maybe, in the wider world out there, people are not all complete c***s." How wrong he was.

I was there, you know, when the shots were fired.
There in my living room with the back boiler on for a bath.
The president, the mall, I saw it all.
I was there, you know, when a man took a giant leap for mankind.
We were all there.

I was there when the bombs went off.
Well, then, or shortly after.
I saw it all. Not live, of course; a recording.
The killing and maiming.
But many of us were there to see that, as it happened.

I was there too, when the wall fell.
Right on top of it, as the people clambered over.
To freedom.
At least half of us saw that.
Many many times I watched that.

I was there when the carriages collided, I saw it all.
At least I think I saw most of it. It might have been a repeat.
I may have been half asleep,
In the heat,
Of the back boiler, on for a bath.

I was not there for the birth, I didn't see any of it.
I was not there to see the living, or the dying and burial
Of the people less important,
Less wealthy,
Less magnificent. Was anyone there to record that?

No one saw their suffering, no one saw it.
No one experienced their hunger.
It wasn't on, was it? Or they didn't show it.
Only the families were there – that died with them,
Without ever entering my living room.

18. THE THREE Rs

At Meaningless Grammar, Dr Nebulas received some excellent school reports. Excellent in that each report book was bound and printed in substitute gold leaf. In each book, his Earth teachers had space to write a paragraph or two of uplifting, spirit-raising and encouraging material.

Every year, though, each box for the most part had just one word in it. It doesn't matter exactly what the word was, 'Satisfactory' abounded – at least eighty per cent of entries just said that. 'Poor' was another. Occasionally, an Earth teacher would render forth a truly creative outburst such as, "this child is a true cretin." Dr Nebulas loved that school. Actually, no, he didn't.

Achievement?
Quite low.
Learning ability?
High.
Melancholy?
Quite often.
But always alive.
In lessons?
Managing.
Assessment?
Is poor.
Too little?
Too late?
Effort?
Give more.
Redemption.
Resentment.
Reality.

19. THE CAREERS MASTER

Dr Nebulas remembers vividly when the time came for him to graduate, if that is the word, from Meaningless Grammar. Interviews were arranged for each student who had previously filled in a form saying what they might like to do. If an Earthling wrote, "I would like to work in industry" and was deemed 'lower class' he would be told to go and get a job in a factory working a drill, or whatever.

If he wrote that he had aspirations to become a scientist and was deemed 'upper class' he would be encouraged to go to university. "Oxbridge only, mind – none of those lefty pinko commie establishments, my lad." Dr Nebulas wrote that he wanted to fly. And heralding from an alien world, as he did, Dr Nebulas already had a pilot's licence.

I sat nervously, at the desk of a man.
A careers master – who said he knew
Of the path an alien should now follow.
It's all mapped out – there – a banker! And all done by interview.

To be a merchant banker?
Oh no, sir! Not I!
I want to fly and soar in the sky.
Oh don't be so ridiculous! And I'll tell you why.

You'd need good sight and fitness,
And four passes won't do.
And you'll need a better upbringing
Than you've been privileged to.

There's no point in seeking
What you really can't have.
Here's an application for banking –
It's really not bad.

I won't take your form, or your silly advice,
And I refuse to become one of those little white mice
Being trampled in the City by bulls and by bears.
I won't join the rat race, as if anyone cares?

About the dream of fulfilment,
In a world lost in shares.
And the price of the stock,
And economic affairs.

I've chosen my own path,
One chosen only by few.
So to be a merchant banker?
No, that really won't do.

20. DIRECTIONS

Dr Nebulas has spent decades researching a social study of life, employment and education on Earth. For many of his formative years, this was a hard journey beset by difficulties and the understanding that he was an alien on this Earth. On one notable occasion, Dr Nebulas was struck by what is called a stolen car.

This is, for those that don't know, an automobile that in fact belongs to someone else, but is broken into and stolen and driven away at speed by some complete fucking c**t. It was silly of him to be standing in the way of this vehicle, Dr Nebulas notes, but there he was one minute obliviously contemplating just what c***s there are on this planet when, all of a sudden, one of them racing at speed to evade capture crashed directly into Dr Nebulas and quite took the edge off of his otherwise unremarkable day.

In fact it has taken many people, who for some reason had no bedside manner, many years and many Earth experiments with probes and sharp instruments to reassemble Dr Nebulas into not quite the same shape and condition that he started in. At the epoch of his formative years, Dr Nebulas noted that several bits of his alien body seemed to have fallen off and others did not seem to be working anymore. A tumble can take many forms, said Dr Nebulas, and you never know when one is coming.

Twenty years along a rocky path there is a junction.
Which way?
Well it's obvious – the hardest way.
Three more years and the pathway ends.
What now? Turn back and start again.
It's a tough path that follows; regroup and assault
On a new path – still rocky – but one that's less fraught.
Eleven more years and the pathway descends
Into darkness, solitude and simple dead ends.
Another new junction, and signs now appear;
Work faster, work harder, your destiny's clear.
Three years of climbing and a summit draws near.
One year of a venture along a new path of hope.
A tumble then follows and the venture is adrift at a stroke.
Flounder for five years and a new path appears,
In the mist of direction, stumble two years.
The mist turns to fog and a foothold is lost,
A crash down through decades; significant cost.
As the fog clears, a realisation that the journey has been
A repetitive struggle along the same pathways first seen.
Direction and distance, but no destination?
An Arcadian dream?
Which way now then?
Well, it's obvious – the hardest way.

21. IRONY

Dr Nebulas was having a bad day at the office when he wrote this one.

Castaway. Gutter. Descent.
Failure. Unpleasantness. Sadness.
Depression. Pain. Solitude.
Disappointment. Lowness. Inability.

Ability. Strength. Tenacity.
Honesty. Loyalty. Generosity.
Talent. Empathy. Willingness.
Contribution. Capability. Potential.

22. DEFORESTATION

Now currently nearing the end of his formative years, Dr Nebulas has realised that he has learned many things. He has found that there are many other living things, such as trees, on this planet that have lived and evolved and survived for hundreds of millennia before man was even here. By contrast, Man is an ephemeral species, here for a fleeting moment in geologic time.

Why is it that no one feels how the tree feels?
As it loses its friends,
As it loses is fight,
As it loses it right
To survive in the forest?

Why is it that the people don't listen?
Or care to mention
The plight and the right and the fight
Of the trees in the forest?

What will it take to defend?
Or rebuild and protect and now mend
The trees in the forest?
We are the trees.

23. THE STRING

Dr Nebulas has realised that, for many Earthlings, life on this planet is about ownership and power. Ownership of goods and property, and power over others. Some on this planet make a considerable contribution to the good of others; philanthropists who are able to punch above their weight, doing so without hope of personal gain. Many other Earthlings have the capability, willingness and experience to contribute, but are prevented from doing so by needless territoriality of information and political power of others over them.

How will I know when it's time?
How will I know when the deed is done?
How will I know when life has run its course?

Good innings?
Best in the long run?
Pegged it at last?

How will I know if I made an impact?
How will I know if anything I did was of any use?
How will I know if what I did was right?

A true success?
Two cars and a detached house?
Made it to the top?

How will I know if I existed at all?
Warmth, appreciation and memory?
Coldness, ingratitude and disregard?

A string unplucked.

24. DRESS CODE

As a research experiment, Dr Nebulas spent some time in the military learning how to kill people. He has often wondered why it is that, paradoxically, certain individuals that he met were given access to awesome weaponry and firepower, and yet were treated as if they could take no responsibility for their actions.

You look disgusting, lad – absolutely disgusting.
But I'm happy in what I am wearing.
Just look at your haircut – your hair, lad – just look at it.
Disgusting – and your father; under his breath he'll be swearing.

We told you at school, lad, the style to adopt.
Short back and sides, lad, and a bit off the top.
That's exactly what I have – and just look at your mop.
And not at some salon, lad, where they charge you a lot.

Am I hurting you, lad? As they say in the army.
What a saying! By REAL men, not like you lad, not smarmy.
In the army they knew, lad; they really knew what to wear.
"On Parade NOW", lad, right smartly,
"Cos I'm standing on your hair!"

Not a pinko, not a leftie, not a hippy, like you, lad.
No Hush Puppies – can you hear me, lad,
With all that hair over your ears?
But uniforms, smartly, "YES SIR! Absolutely!" Lad
Was all that us short-haired young squaddies would hear.

My hairstyle is comfortable; in a style of my choosing,
And I'm saddened by the complaints, the bullying and abusing
Of my character, at my age? Is there no way to relate?
To me – an individual; not an institution inmate.

25. LARKIN' ABOUT

It is nearly the end of Dr Nebulas' formative years and as a product of his alliance with love-of-his-life alien, he now has an alien offspring of the female kind. Now this female alien is awesome. She's adventurous, beautiful (just like love-of-his-life alien) and with a tenacious appetite for voyage and discovery.

This offspring has ventured to the four corners of planet Earth, explored every continent, trekked through rainforest, expeditioned to the South Pole, skydived from great heights. And she has had her passport, camera and all her possessions nicked by, as she tactfully put it, "some complete thieving c**t" on an island a thousand miles from anywhere in the South China Sea. She is, to a great extent, a chip off the old alien.

Second love-of-his-life alien has been taught by Dr Nebulas and love-of-his-life alien that voyages of discovery come at a price – but that it's a price worth paying.

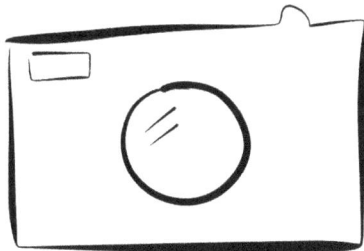

Your mum and dad, they fuck you up? That's bad?
But is it through all the faults they had?
Mine have shown me that I could fly
And how I could live, and how I could die.
They told me that it's OK to take a big chance,
To make a difference; go out on a limb.
Live life to the full; carpe diem.

So, girl, when you fuck it up some day
Then that's all right – you felt the fear, and did it anyway,
And that's OK.
Because your mum and dad, girl, they know
That life's for living; so go girl go!
And when there's an almighty mess,
Don't worry, girl – you did your best.
So pick yourself up and start again
On some other adventure – it's never in vain.

It is not in the belief that we do dangerous things
Because we think we are immortal.
We do them because we know we are NOT immortal.
One day, girl, you'll be a parent yourself
And, like you, with a daughter with spirit; in a world to be had.
So you can tell her it's not YOUR fault she fucked up bad,
But it's all been the fault of her gran and grandad.

26. WISHFUL THINKING

On a cold rainy day, Dr Nebulas ponders what it would be like if he could have anything he wanted. He contemplates that, even without personal wealth and power, his life is rich already. He is wealthy in other ways; rich in relationships, rich in imagination and rich in experience.

If you were given three wishes
What would they be?
For unlimited wealth?
Or to end poverty?

Would you wish to be thinner?
Or fitter? Or fatter?
Would you wish for more power?
Would that simply not matter?

Would you make a wish for yourself?
And a wish for another?
A wish for mankind?
Or a child and a mother?

Would you wish to end all wars?
A wish to end pain?
For power and glory?
For personal gain?

Two wishes for indulgence?
One wish for repentance?
A wish for forgiveness?
Or to end a long sentence?

Would you wish all men equal?
To make them all brothers?
Except for yourself; of course,
Who would be more equal than others.

What would I wish for if given three wishes?
The first wish would be
That I were not given
Three wishes.

27. THE GREAT DIVIDER

Dr Nebulas has noticed that urbanisation has generated some interesting by-products of the class structure. Consumption cleavages have given rise to target hardening and class fortifications.

There seems to be a passion
To live; according to a fashion,
In cul-de-sac communities of class.

These territorial utopia
Where neither you nor I go,
House residents used to living under glass.

Here, the common elements
Are kept at-bay by settlements,
Who fortify their walls and property.

These echelon and gentry
Own butler, guard, and sentry,
Who know their place and must act properly.

A place of wealth and capital
Where occupiers, dash it all,
Don't care for the unwashed lower class

At St Peter's they'll be queuing
And He may not be letting you in
At heaven's gates; He may not let you pass.

28. BASE METALS

In his penultimate poem, Dr Nebulas ponders the things that Earthlings should value, but seemingly do not. In a post-apocalyptic world, the real riches of the planet have been lost to worthless re-incarnated ingots.

I used to walk along a metal path:
Autumn gold
Silver birch
Platinum skies
Copper beech
The path has given way to a metal road
With eyes that glow
And metal carriages that thunder by.
What has become of the base metals?

29. YOU LOST ME AT HELLO

Dr Nebulas has become an affectionado of both people and real ale, but not necessarily at the same time. He tells me that he often spends his Earth evenings as a lonely philosopher, melancholically contemplating a hostile world. "Why is it," he retorts, "seriously, that people can be such complete c***s." Dr Nebulas fears that he will never know.

Two pints of your best, bartender, if you would.
And the bartender obliged, as a bartender should.

An evening at the local evolved into a night at the boozer,
With a footballing crowd and a goalkeeping bruiser.

A mistake of my clothing? A choice of deep blue.
The blue of the fans – damn – now a deafening hue.

HELLO! HERE'S ANOTHER! A SUPPORTER LIKE US!
No I really don't think so, but I don't make a fuss.

The conversation revolved around fuckin' headars and footars,
On a paginated pitch where the text doesn't matter.

An alien world, which is simply not cricket.
Like the footie, there's a ball, but no goal; just a wicket.

Ebullience flowed like the beer from the barrel.
The evening wore on and the fans wore less apparel.

A heaving mass regaled a fuckin'-certain goal that was missed.
The bartender apologised – that they're really all pissed.

Some guy was a dribbler, another had passed it.
Their goalie was a fuckin'-wanker, and ours was FANTASTICCC.

So, footie? A confusing game, with a language oblique.
They lost me at hello; I'm not part of their clique.

Epilogue: POEMS BY AN ALIEN, Part Deux?

OK, so Nebby has just been informed by his publishers that until he 'gets his finger out' and starts writing the second part of his series of poems, then the first part will, most likely, not be published. This would be sad, not just for Nebby, but for the hoards of Earthlings waiting to share his joy. It would also be bad for his publishers who have, in fact, negotiated, if that is the word, a 'win-win, yellow hat, blue sky thinking, fifty percent commission'. And they will get totally fuck all if they don't get it published pronto.

Mind you, Nebby surmised, the publishers suggested charging seven pounds and ninety-nine pence of Earth money for the 'Part Un' book to each Earthling daft enough to want a copy; so it would need at least a million daft Earthlings to make Nebby and his publishers anything like the amount of money they need to maintain their habits...

So, Nebby has suggested (not unreasonably, he felt) that 'Part Un' should be sold at seven million, nine hundred and ninety thousand pounds and, that way, there only has to be just one daft sod with a few quid knocking about to buy it, then we'd all be happily heading off to the chemist... In Nebby's mind, there is a reason for this pricing mechanism...

After all, recently Dr Nebulas and 'love-of-his-life' alien pilgrimaged to the metropolis to see an art exhibition containing, amongst other shit, a bloody great dawb of some tart with her tits hanging out, holding onto what appeared to be a basket of melons. Neb reports that the sitter's face was, quite frankly, a bit on the dodgy side and he was unable to fathom why on Earth the artist, who apparently drove a Transit, put her nose where it was. Just odd.

Love-of-his-life alien, on the other hand, told Nebby that this gallery viewing of an Old Master was a true honour, and that he now needed to "grow up !"and "conceptualise", to try and understand the deeper emotions felt by the artist as he wrestled to portray his feelings on canvas. Well, Nebby was lost. His only recollections of Old Masters were the c***s at Meaningless Grammar School who had tried to teach him, or rather, beat the shit out of him, and Nebby felt that he had already conceptually wrestled to portray them in his poems.

Now, although not qualified as an Earthling-recognised art critic – you know the type – shiny jacket, cravat, supercilious and dribbling sneer and condescending air...Or, as Nebby puts it, another flowery twat with an opinion...Nebby nonetheless is always prepared to proffer a view.

So, he said, although no doubt enthusiastically penned by the artist, this dawb of a tart with melons conceptually suggested to Nebby that the artist was probably just getting any old crap down on canvas as quickly as he could so that he could then relentlessly shag the sitter before her mother arrived to take her back to school. Apparently that was all the rage in those days.

Nebby's alternate hypothesis, though, suggests that the sitter in the painting might, in fact, truly have been an old slag – fucking ugly as sin, with her ear re-pinned to her shoulder after a bar brawl – and up for a bit of oil paint and a shag later.

Either way, the painting was not to Nebby's liking, even more so when the annoying uniformed git sitting in the gallery corner informed Neb that this painting was worth over sixteen million pounds, and that he should keep all of his four hands off it – in case he were to leave some sort of slime.

Sixteen million? Sixteen million? For a dawb of a tart with melons? Well, Nebby was dumbfounded and sent a message to his publishers to immediately change the cover picture of his 'Part Un', from a picture of a Rhodesian Ridgeback dog eating eight strawberries, to a 'tart with lemons' or, as it is in vogue these days to write everything in French, a 'tarte citron'.

Now, a picture of a 'tarte citron' on the front cover, Nebby surmised, must be worth a few quid. "Oh" Nebby also added to the publishers, "shove a nose in the citron!"

That should do it.

www.ingramcontent.com/pod-product-compliance
Lightning Source LLC
Chambersburg PA
CBHW071932020426
42331CB00010B/2831